Contents

The Taste Of Orange

To anyone who wants to see the world not only with their own eyes, but also with a sparkle of someone else's

I dedicate this book to you all.

INTRODUCTION

Why I am writing this book and what led me to it.
So, nice from the beginning, about 6 years ago, I started writing one of my first books called California. It was a lot of fun to watch after those few years how my style changed and overall how I changed. And that's why I want to take this book in a slightly different direction. For example, I would like to write poetry

poetry that is not just ordinary. And that's why I created this book

The first book

Because autumn is coming, the first book will be about this beautifully colored season

I.

the sun
    Gold orange sun visible at every
corner of morning window.

You'll know the feeling that thinks about
the darkness every dawn.
DARK DAWN
so tender, We waiting for the spark of
what we used to see. What was and is no
longer.
and the further the time, the darker the
dawn and shadowy sky

II.

light, yellow burning light

                    Luminance of a candle
that is burning on my desk at the moment.

gentle scent emerging
          In tiny space.

In room which,
which is small, little.

how can a candle burn?

Blaze like the monumental fire
          Burn in lamps.
oh, mystery.

III.

I induct the vision in my head

reflection of falling leaves
which I could retell.

dimming life o'
leaves? have been long since falling from
voluminous trees.
   Ordinary trees!
rainless.
but with a fragment of a tint.
only minor mention of their past moments
A point of life.

MAK
YO

IV.

the olden days. not so long ago
lavender fields-pastures saturated in
purple tint
where the violets bloomed

bloomed so dense
that eyes suddenly began to breathe
        Eyes drawn in breath
The feeling no longer WILL BE!
behindhand.
so far that the sun will see the earth
tiny as a grain of sand.
That soon it will absorbs the whole space

                    Absorb space.

V.

the origin.
Origin of THE end
                    that REVEAL what only
mortals see. Plain beings.
unaware of
world,
    Only word at the end of judgement.
a sentence allied from a few letters in
tiny words are

nothing else

Just a plain ends in the beginnings.

4Y4L W UHO
T7LP
G N4
W4YA
HOR
T7L

VI.

Pure dark,
          feeling when we're not sure
what could happen.
               When the light is just like
a short flash.
gratefulness of light, everything exist.
everything that darkness sees and the
eyes don't catch
They'r givin' the light to a shadow.
                    To a shadow of lies

VII.

Cold,
The pressure that tell you to stay warm.
feeling
which is not written. gentle touch.
a touch that does a lot.
How can describe what can't be seen by
    Mortal eyes. Can we think about anyway?

The question pays attention. To an
Ordinary words
Forcing cold.

VIII.

orange poems, orange.
not only that
not only autumn is colored
orange.
it will no be as it was, cold,
different. So different and at the same
time the same. as strong, as it can be,
so tender and cold.

orange. Orange grows in the heart of
autumn.
tones line those
shapes that float in the air, you can
hear only subtle sound of rustling.

colorful sound of
autumn.

IX.

         honey,
sweet.
So sweet.
not like a bee. Like a bee that
just appear at hive.
honeycombs. Smoker.
Gently overflows,

                                        so

slowly and quietly.
spills over our lives. It sweetens our
life by every second it falls.
Yore bitter.

bitter life.

X.

Purple. Purple as the deepest sea,

lies in stony middle,
                    lies in silence, in
winter.
shows the beauty of colors when others
are sleeping.
In the light of darkness, in the hot
cold,
during short days.
It's showing colors.

XI.

swim in a drop of water. Art?
No? What to give, I will.
go somewhere
        somewhere in the unknown.
      Where no one has ever been before.

and is it unique? To go there ?

I think no ?

XII.

Moonlight Mirror.
do you know ? that The shine,
It's just a reflection. maybe yellow.
The shadow, the big shadow, determines
the direction. the direction of
moonlight.
     12. Number twelve, so simple, but even
so complicated and at the same time,
Simple.
Ordinary? no.
and so translucent
Or invisible at other times?
The sun is shining, the sky is left by a
sign. Signature.

          Signature of the moonlight.

XIII.

     Orange peel. With cloves!
Orange, once different.
Thin, but hard. Bitter, but sweet.
fragrance. Moves the rooms.
The sweet scent washes away their
corners.
Subtle ginger, a taste that everyone
knows.
Known, for ages.

orange peel with cloves

XIV.

I see an orange moon. orange moon
during the day while life awakens.
where is the fire did it got lost? They
covered it!
the slightly dark atmosphere beats hard.
so strong that every single eye sees how
it wakes up.
In that cold, in that fall.
so majestic large fields. Once inhabited
different types of plants. Not anymore.
the great cold prevents them from moving,
to come out from the eyes to the world.
So gentle
such a gentle smooth movement would
suffice. But no. Time is time when it
ticks right. Tic. tac.
    when there is no time. There is no
cold. No beautiful flowers, plants,
fields. when there is no time. There
isn't a single flash or even a tiny
orange moon that stood out a moment ago
on the sky.
There is no moon now. There is no time to
say yes. which would put out the fire.
stopped the water.
Spoken yes. No hours ticking.
Only yes. not a single trace of life.
time has stopped and so have we.

XV.

Days. the shortened days that darkness
had seized into its hateful hands, the
light seen of a great star shining alone.
It shines so alone. clouds show its
beauty in the seas of the sky. in the
dense seas of sky, straight to the oceans
that suddenly release. they release drops
that start to tremble in
light stellar fumes.
they will dance until they fall.
They will fall and fall until the earth
tell enough.
they start making knocking sounds in the
silence of the darkness. the sound of
falling.
like ticking the clock.
Ticking strong but weak at the same time.
they form a group of water. water that
glows in the dark with the lights and
colors of night.
like a stealer. The mirror that the Earth
created from the oceans above us. to make
the beautiful be noticed.
Created by drops of the oceans. So big.
so blue. So deep. like drops.
                drops of the oceans.

Bittersweet Cinnamon

This book was a really fast paced written script because I got a bit blocked by the winter.

INTRODUCTION

I had planned this book to be so sweet and gentle, but by the time I was writing it I was starting to feel very differently and that's part of the reason I had not finished this book.

I had not originally planned to publish it, but at least I edited this version in response to people's suggestions.

The second book

The second book as I mentioned will be about winter mood and will be less hectic. Because everything is silent in winter.

I.

        The space.
Void of meaning in life, is so
noiseless ?   So mere.
        Yet it will come one day. Time will
come to life's bristling space. As if no
snowflake has fallen. Not needing it, but
wanting it. That's different
                In the spirit as it
came so it will go. Coolness and
darkness. Directions we know nothing
about are coming.

This dark & bright will shift to other
shores. The soul's happiness chill boils
with delight just like ours. with a
sadness that makes us want to close the
three-month long window with the head
upside down.
        A chill to bring joy suddenly makes
the harbor come alive,
                By the cold

II.

           the sensation of thoughts.
                                   those
empty ones
that fled at will.
Each touch dissolves time into reality.
       To be centered. Going slowly to
places
which have no purpose.
                 The accidental dream
In the presence
       Of Destiny
       By which day they flare up. Being
light, warmth,
A fire that warms the feelings and makes
the empty moments of dark days come
alive, into something as beautiful as the
air.   Bursts foth to life in its moments
an' tenses of time.
                 where the stars conquer the
world till only that light survives in
the mind of the city,
                       The fortune in
worlds of stars

III.

    one sees
Another hears
       Fifth Sense
   There's No World Without a Bit of
Life In Which Destiny Falls into the Ash.
Shifting upon a leaf in your dreams
Bound by the the tale of a sun, of life
where only the dark is made alive by
light. The purple tinge of dreams passes
to us.

IV.

The seas of crowds. Delicate words
floating in immense spaces.
          the sensation of tingles. Unaware,
perhaps
But the lights lending sleep to the
darkness. Otherwise the eye doesn't
seeing the depths of the oceans that are
buried.
                    Reflections in glass
mirrors never lie. What they see they
will reveal. No, it doesn't disguise, it
reveals the silent mind.
                    that in the
Distant harbour those last distinct bits
of mist.
The mists set the world in movement. It
climbs, it sinks, it swings from side to
side.
                    hiding its face in the
narrow places in the bushes. In the
creeping corners of the eye. Impossibly
but intimately alive.
In a moment of words a thought passes
that will not remain a mirage. The
sensation swayed by the sound of a wave
tells a story. Stories of mist and
mirrors that see each other worlds of
mind in bits.
                In which words are absent to
tell the silence.
Of the unmistakable darkness which it
draws,
                    Light
                        of the
crowds

V.

Waves of hearing
From the sound of the breeze they will
fly away.
Where each one forms a sea.   The
wind over the waves - creating
                         diamonds
that
Diamonds that furrow the worlds of fate,
by sheer chance, as if a feather of fate
had waved a thought.
                Water that purifies
chance and ignites the power of the
world's oceans.
        Rising in the feeling of freedom,
in the power of the great and mighty
worlds.

Time passes, swallowing every drop that
ticks on the windows of houses.

It will roll in waves full of tails that
will bring fates preoccupied with
thoughts.

Spring Blooms

I want to dedicate this book to spring itself, because it is underestimated.

INTRODUCTION

Waiting for the moments of spring days in the subtle reflections of old memories, I am writing this book. Winter shows us how cold it is, without life. After winter comes a beautiful period of awakening, a time of spring. When the joy is overflowing with the colors that are seen through the delicate green leaves, flowers and scents. Enjoy this season as well as my book.

The third book

Time when life bloom in air

Dance of Colors

The reflection of the moonlight in the
pools of rain, hovering above the clouds.

 I love when cherries bloom, the scent
reflects love, enthusiasm, the power to
live. The feeling of hovering gives us
spring sparkle.
 A gentle breeze floods every orange
sunset.
 A touch of tea vapor accompanies the
harmonies at the end of each spring day.
The view from the window plays the
orchestra in nature. Sounds, colors,
smells play in our senses music of
feelings, the tenderness of sound that we
do not hear.
 Yellow daffodils and red tulips play the
violin. Purple violets and white daisies
on small drums.
 The trees with green leaves reflect life
in the beauty of nature.
 Pulling the forces of life, the
inexpressible emotions of happiness and
good mood.

Color drops (underappreciated love)

butterfly, frame that hangs on the wall.
Butterfly wings, rainbow colors reflect
smiles at the memory of beauty, tangible
moments on the horizon.
  Horizons of white dust turn into yellow
fields, as colorful and sweet as the
moments before us, as sweet as the spring
sunrise. I sing awakening nature with
birds, illuminated by the rays of the
sun. The spring rain glistens like
crystal drops reviving velvety colors and
scents. in the air you can feel the love
she gives us, nature itself.
The love that people don't see

Not enough

I don't know the depth of the words, the
language makes my task difficult. I put
indescribable feelings in ordinary words.

 Sometimes we are not enough. How to
describe a feeling to be understood when
familiarity with words is
straightforward. That endless feeling
and the power of emotions is
misunderstood for me several times. Poor
language, nothing more than a tool for
material things. pain trying to do
something more.

Desire is a need,
for a moment to speak,
word in a dream,
smile is a seam.
Shortness of breath,
is just a feel for me,
to be seen. by eyes of thee

Vibrant calling's

spring reflections? colored pieces of
fragmented life. darkness without
feeling afraid. The birth of sweet
moments.

 Metaphors of sounds and color
reflections, a flowering life of joy.
Did I mention daisies? So beautiful
flowers!
 Singing with love.
 Songs of emotions that fly in the wind
of thoughts about winter. a snowdrop so
tender in such a cold cloak wakes up.

That beauty is beautiful
 gives us hope
 feelings of false change
 they arouse fear.
 Bright lilies show that beauty
 she is beautiful. when life after the
cold
 comes to life. can and will
believe
 in days, full of rays of color

My constant dreams

I am constantly waiting for the moments
when my ideas and dreams come true.When
the feather of freedom flies out. Age, a
number expressing time. But that time,
so important. How old do we have to be
for society to recognize us?
 I am constantly waiting for moments
where society will only help and live,
not an authority of importance. Where
the law recognizes emotion. Where people
will not just be a machine gears.
 I am constantly waiting for the times
when people will be flowers. Flowers
that have a goal, flowers that grow that
they feel. They show beauty and move the
corners of the mouth upwards. So
innocent, beautiful and tender.
 I am constantly waiting for the times
when people will be human. When feelings
and behaviors will be recognized and
respected.
        I am constantly waiting for moments
when I will not constantly wait.

Ruling mornings

Mornings,
 bright morning after days of darkness.
 When dark moments are shorter than
before. Days pass without frost, golden
rays fill spaces and enchant smiles.
 The days seem longer.
 The nights are still dark and dark.

 When I see how beautiful the sun is, I
feel like sitting on the window and
watching. Feel the beauty that comes
 feel happy without bad moments

The breath of new suns

Days go by, like flowers bloom. The world
moves to the driest shore, time to time
sun
beams show but the bloom is what we
waiting for.
  I lust for life for my dreams to shine
through the love. The moment of light in
my heart.
For memories to come, for thoughts to
come, the heat of sunny days.
For the brightest of those nights till
morning sun in early times. On those
routes in the middle of our paths.
So I love to think of those past times
till the future days of new possibilities
that make my smile shine. The people
around to be no sadder, no more off.
Turned to new minds, to better selves.
To be understood.

The silver bee

The shine of ring *a.bird for ode* to sing in open windows. I see wind, the storm in rainy day.
Soul left my eye when the sun shined just for a day. The warm in sun will come till the end. Cycling time dividing *moon and sun* between hours of fun. Could you tell time if there were *no clock* in sight. Could you tell if the hour is on an open window ? Could you tell the rain to come back on later days.

      the felling lost in verses of timeless days. The <u>concept</u> of vision in hot awareness of the reality **between us**. Till the night comes to see, to fell the cold breath of *falling* sun on our necks. I love to see a heat of *waves* in these later spring day. To see the silver bee that bring luck and joy to the heart in a port of madness. Hello, I said to the window when sun said bye.

Cloudy in my mind

Why are the ports so strong, the sails so
fragile. All eyes are on the ships. The
sheet looks so simple and hides the depth
of colors and patterns. The unknown
clouds into which it plunges and sinks
into it once. The wood of the ship keeps
her from going down, to shine, and to
show that she too can be bright,
colorful, and flowering.Unable to
describe her colors, she does not always
see them, if so so vaguely. Why is the
ship floating in the darkness, why is it
sinking its sail? If she didn't have to,
but does she? She has a problem, maybe
something is holding her or someone just
tied her to the extra rope, and by
letting him go, she is afraid that she
will be different, that she will go in a
different direction and people will start
looking at her. Maybe the colors will
change, maybe the material. Should he
release the rope? Maybe she can't do it
alone or someone can hold the rope.
Although she doesn't mind. She shines
with her colors anyway. Maybe it will be
better if the rope stays where it is,
because maybe it won't tie the tension
there then.

Moonrise

Why the sun rises above the horizons? The
shine that wake up all life, the colors
of life.
On the other side a night is dark. I
don't like dark nights. Only when the
moon is full it shines down in the middle
of dark.
A day in spring is like art to me.
                         b*RING* me
joy by arts of nature in long days.

by Arts forming in our sight .
                Thanks to the nature
itself.
                I see moon*rise* on a sunny
day when the sun is not alone,
                the sign of night is
now just a day.
A bright sunny day.

After the storm

After every storm comes light, sun,
something beautiful.
The fear of the unconscious leaves us
tempted, we wait and wait for the moments
when it passes.
What if a storm is not so bad, what if we
don't have to worry about it, when we
know its consequences.
The rain will sprinkle the earth, which
will grow and show us beauty, even such a
dark storm can bring good things, the
sun's rays blooming among the still dark
clouds
After every storm, something comes after
fear passes.

Sparkling Green

A book about the poetry of words across seasons, spanning both summer and spring. This book is dedicated to everything natural that lives and grows from the earth

INTRODUCTION

"My spring reflections gradually, but surely, intertwine with spring, adorned with both big and small smiles. The days are not yet counted, but everyone already knows where time is heading. The leaves on the trees have spoken their piece. The weather only confirms that the time of summer is approaching. Enjoy it wholeheartedly."

The fourth book

Or the season of summer beginnings and spring and spring endings

Green poems

I.

Like a wind in the air
So soft and weak on a early day
Like a sun, flying in the hair
I see wind with storms incoming
The rain will dance around our
Sanctuary, the waters of the sky
The heart intact from influence

II.

Walks of raindrops on the yellow cloak of
fields,
Through windows full of rain, gloomy
spring weather
Flashes before my eyes, reflections of
spring in puddles along the road express
joy in indescribable words.
7:35 - Demandice, a bus standing on the
road, in which I am. It proceeds to its
next stop. It has a clear goal, not
stopped by rain, storm, cold, or warmth.
It reaches its destination, concludes the
journey, and begins anew.

III.

Miles Long, the heat. Morning tree that
felt in dribble of billions shiny drops
in edges of rainbows. Window, shine of
moon in tiny reflection of stars. Earth
at the edge of power. The stalagmite in
depths of caves, a caveman showing
respect, mining. Crystals borrowing, deep
in earth. Tiny homes and large cities.
Rivers, lakes the blue and green dancing
across grey tall buildings.

Yellow poems

I.

The gleam of bells, the gaze of a thousand lights. Day by day. Words sparkling across the horizon. Moon like May. Time like pictures, small moments in life. Walks through narrow pathways. Darkness behind the light. Touches of paper in the wind. Sky blue, like seas in summer nights.

II.

The pink sky, glistened above red cloud
after golden hour. Warm horizons moving,
just a bit of waves from the ocean. The
heirloom of sun, the moon flickering from
dark purplish gate to sky. One
reflection, a million tiny lamps
levitating around it. Seeing what has
been hidden. Singing what hasn't been
heard. Tilting till the sky goes fully to
dark blue. Till no eyes will see. Till no
owl will be. In dark summer night

III.

The sky went off, cloud glimmered around
heavy rain. Drops, where each one is no
so clear to speak about. Where each one
is so heavy, mindless throughs coming up
when staring at it.
Melodies of random sounds a feeling like
lost in breeze of time, same as thee I
was. Same as rain. Heaviness of life came
up and then disappeared like that one
glistening drop. be you like you see thee
in mirrors, beautiful, sparkling with
glamour but still different. Not as
others

Blue poems

I.

It's that time. time of the year when day
shines across land for more than just
4X6x60"
Carpets of moss, where water flows like a
spring on stones. stems of green flower
parts flying in the air. "The wind, the
hail's coming," said. Thee build houses
nor helping, breaking. the health's way
only curved could be, le em do it. Let me
knew it, that spots are indifferent.
pursuant flowers have yellowish-colored,
perfectly shaped petals trying.
Nor i see anything. Cant I be,
indefinitely by others? stroms breaking
laws. causing wounds to already wounded
victims. be thee be me. Do what yee will
and thee may shine a smile on yee. trust
in it. Fell into the channel switch in
the wind.

II.

TILL THE ENDLESS TRAGEDY

A seed was born in the fastest storm
the flow was deep. Like the
ocean sirens sang as the pirates
lived. Bravery is movement no no like
other. Who died in the hottest summers
like men in wars. As the kings
on their thrones. I lived to see.
HOW dreadful bravery can
be. Like a slave to death, you'll be !

III.

The world is wild place to be in, you
must just see right through it
Might I Moore, might I see don't mind ME!
I'm just a little soldier in this endless
war and the World is bored to see
more, to see the wild in our hearths. To
be in waters that pave deep in the hidden
course of fear. To be a traveller to see
World. Not working forevermore. Pave your
path amongst these thorns, pave the way
among the hearts. Win the tribute of the
past and move with the future like a
blast.
Love to live, Love to be! in this endless
eternity

MAYHEM WITH DAVE

A series of poems

Deep talks

Once I dreamed, like a reality it seemed
to be.
Once the bitter hour strikes, it moves us
like dolls in house,
The one the second and ending at the
witchy hour.
Things or opinions like rewinding, the
behavior of the moment.
Why ? the question asked, but after a
dream. The question sits down At the lap
of the past.
The
unchangeable history, like a moment in
time, i seamed
So small and not remembered, like the
thoughts of mine weighted only tons of
Feathers. Like a dull anvil. A leviathan
from the deep oceans. I never forget how
Strong was to not think. Never...

Alone

There once was a time, I felt so off. The
sky of thunder lay behind my doors.
Take it easy as it seems. I dunno what to
do, what to say. How it sounds.
Once I'm alone, I'm like a fbi hunting
the criminal. Finding clues for one hour.
Go to the lab till the second will strike
on the clock. Then investigate onto
fourth, nothing
Else to do. The world is so quiet, then a
scream and repeat the round, begin the
round.

Lost in feeling

The mind is telling you to stop, to move
like a neighborhood. In the shiny new
street
Of new Amsterdam, where i have never
been. Like war and peace. A newly opened
To a world of opportunities. I've never
had one. Such a dose. In my feeling i was
lost, cooperate One to each other, the
time of hurting it was, like another
being, like a mind in prison.
Stolen by a robber whose target was
repeating time to time again.
But there was nothing else.
No such emotion, nor happiness.

After light

The party was hot, the dance of millions
of shiny stars, the light that fades
every night.
After mourn it comes the dew. The point
where a new bottle is ready to be filled.
A drop like lightning struck. The new
way, new path was moving me forward.
To unknown land full of mysteries. Be
heard I once dreamed of, be listened I
once
dreamed of. But I find it more exhausting
than just wandering in millions of tiny
chances.
Once it was good, once bad. Sometimes it
also hurts.

But I recovered, bravely.

Pale

Cold September nights, like a winter
freeze. Just like it. I saw many things.
I felt many more.
I kissed a dream. I sang a song, like I
was under a pale moon but it was blood.
From nowhere.
Tiny glistening golden dots, not stars,
but light from the city below us. Felt
like immortals.
From light to dark, from sun to cold. The
warmth of bodies like never before. Not
only that was shown. In that night of
cold and dark skies, I felt fire by the
kiss of his lips. Pale i was no more.

Sparkling

Earth begins to drop her chestnuts, clock stared into my mind. How it is. How is that possible? How to breathe under the dusk. I went to look in the past.
I saw the grief in my lust. My mind turned around. I'lll never feel that anymore. Like a captain I felt like a new ship was sent to me. New map to a bigger island where the treasure island I've never seen, was all the time. I never saw another way, another path like I see now. From now on, my smile is real.

FAETFULL POEMS

A series of poems

Shimmer & Stone

My dreams, like oak & bird ashes flought
into the wind. The roots caught the dirt
as I spoke to Earth.
The wind in trees, the wind in a bush
like a ship on sea till a wave pass. As
the sunset strikes noon and the water
drops the spoon, endless cycle that will
fall into the night of a scattered storm.
In the eye as wind and down like a
shimmer & stone.

White Chocolate

A channel on the road, terra blue, the
face of the lightest fae. Spring blooms
as I wrote seem too late to show. Live in
an oracle, and see the truth. Trust the
way, as I trust you. Pave the path of the
wicked hut. Be my first-morning star on
my little sky. Kiss like candy on a
stick. Eat me like your white chocolate.

Drawer Fight

Wood and planks, table bonds. Under my
legs for me.
Dance of shards and sounds of cracks. In
the dream of worms and ants. Desk to hang
my portraits bet. Like ash, it
disappeared. I am a toy for their final
fight in the club. Locked between drawers
and little chairs.

Island of fireflies

A blink of light passed me by. The end of
my thousand life. I don't wanna end me,
just enlighten me I saw the truth and
changed the past. They saw my ignition,
fear no more how to go on and on they
asked, into the silent hills of lust as
the spring on hot, like a night on a
stove.
Breathe herbs, do not refuse my offer it
is quite a jewel so take it like you
would take me into the pool. Swim like a
shark behind his obstacles, catch me like
the flu and won my heart on the island of
fireflies.

Our Sakura leaf

Roses & bloom dried to tell how it would be. How beautiful the sun Il shine, how gorgeous the rain is. Every color is Saturated as a filter in Photoshop. Days pass by like trains on tracks as the music plays. Sakura flowers will shine every year like the cycle of life and love. To celebrate colors in every shade. To make & draw a smiley face next to a hearth. When every shadow is Just black on white. Every scene in the club is just an art. My heart broke with the drama. Let it shine with a smile on my face with pink, white blossom leaf.

mirror reflections of myself

Sprinklers & ram, they have seen the
pain.
The longest you work, the hardest it is.
One drip of water, another of blood. Why
is too much a frog that has caught a fly
in its tongue? How to fake the view is
how close the houses are, how close the
view now in this world, like a reflection
of someone else. Why stare? Why so silent
now? No sorry, no more.
Live in my garden now, and I take care of
it. any dead plant I pick up. I put in
the trash for not taking place & energy.
be the death plant to my garden now. or
the dreams you have will shatter from my
reflection in shards of the sea that
droughts them to salt.

BIRD, NET & SKY

My nature, like I mature changes like a
summer sky, like a winter sunset from old
to youth I am drowning. Free like a bird
that has seen the world. Wrong people in
the wrong positions, bad influence and
deadly worlds. One hint and 8 billion
minds. Nothing changed the feeling
closed, like before on my cafe table like
down in the rain and the cold through
burning. Don't speak don't talk to
yourself go sleep. Wake up and do it all
over again. Be the tunnel and the deep
sea of drowned. Do not listen be face to
face its warning

LIKE BEE THAT TOLD MY STORY

One more night, like an ode to rain. The Moore, the swamp. Deep lakes on the fire horizons drought-like summer. Spring said goodbye as the beat bloomed. See the sun like I see the wind. Like water that has caught the web of dreams. Bee sat on my front doorstep. Told me bout a liquor of yellow gold that swims in jars. Told me bout the home of flies about cold winters and the end of lives. As the sun sets at night my face smiled cuz a memory of mine from the first time when we met appeared in my mind. how i saw you like a baby bee that has seen the hive for the first time, golden scenes full of glitter in its eyes, wipe them off and starts to fly. The first beam of light passed me by in front of my eyes.

A series of poems

CAUSE I CARE

One day, i saw stars.
Sparkling.
When there was no light furthermore I
believed. It turned into nothing.
When the sky was falling slower than
ever. Then Hope came.
When one day better than ever my smile
came. The nights were cold. The summer
odd. In mid of falling leaves i felt
butterflies in my cheeks and as the bloom
got yellowish i know I'm in right space
and time to be loved.

Why do I always slip

What came before me, storm rain or
hurricanes. I Live by being a someone.
The highs the lows. Counting stars till I
see the sun, counting days till I fell
breeze of sparks. Now standing or lying
next to a mirror seems so off. Why it
hurts when I need smile in every
butterfly. My mind making things up
before making a choice.
Opinions abandoned like morality, every
color after sun, every second till
morning.
Why do I always slip. Why my fortune
teller broke the ball. A coin, dropped in
fountain. Will it change anything?
At least I can try.

ABOVE, DOWN THE PACIFIC

Like vines and dignity
an air in liquidy run through narrowed
paths, roots breathing skin dripping,
boiling the water be Oh!
Running like electricity.
Those the high may shire as warm summer
wine.
Thus the morn' mist carries the light
featheral feels.
In all the luxury you sparking be till
night sky flooded be by stars, anise
rising from a cup, flicking of green &
red lights,
pacific to my stream like film never
ending

In the wind there's a beauty

Exalted dreams and possibilities, blue
outcomes with spark. Beneath earth &
dust, they fought. Pebbles ring on a
shiny water lake when no cabin is built
by man. When no foggy instrument, near
the surface hidden truth, unacceptable
and honorable majesty with throne from
concrete where pastry & blood occur,
heals the rotten wounds of humanity by
false higher power, There lies the beauty
of innocence, where justice cries in a
flow of tears. The home is a sacred place
to be; the home lies in hearts of pride
and paradise. The home is not a place;
the home is an emotional form of love in
many variables.

A firecracker

A sound of waves in distant horizons,
Though burning night and in-lighted
evening
A words like songs singing and birds
humming
Weight of rain and stone cold wind where
candles burned on midnight street
Punch a pile sucking dirt that bothered
Pin the hardest faith
The board be singing like the birds
Flashing aurora rise above the pin board
Like when it rains just for a second I
remember
To always be kind even if not

Where I am

Where I am is a place not quite the place you call home rather than some house on the street.
Where I am is nothing and something at the same time. The wide trees and overgrown fields where blooming sunflowers live. Not quite the place you could call, not quite the city where you feel. Just a thought that I might quite be living in your heart wholeheartedly you're mine with every autumn leaves and even sunsets. With every bubbles in blue sparkling lakes. Indefinitely apart from reality. A place called love.

White Beauty

A flower to me is a flower to be
Like our spirit fought the dust, like our
Bodies bring the shards, crystal clean
Is to live beneath heavenly viragos
lives.
The feelings of them, seemingly
constructing
bridges. To be hear nor seen in attic of
thee
Like a dusk to dust from those winter
leaves
Like a white sage that has never saw the
snow.
How miraculous to be entitled with her.

At least I can try.

What came before me, storm rain or
hurricanes. I Live by being a someone.
The highs the lows. Counting stars till I
see the sun, counting days till I fell
breeze of sparks. Now standing or lying
next to a mirror seems so off. Why it
hurts when I need smile in every
butterfly. My mind making things up
before making a choice . Opinions
abandoned like morality, every color
after sun, every second till morning. Why
do I always slip. Why my fortune teller
broke the ball. A coin, dropped in
fountain. Will it change anything? At
least I can try.

Rigid clouds, sun's burning down

At the loop i swing so high
Times like olden skies
Suns burning down where
Ya see only tranquil breeze
Setting hours passing by
Because I couldn't stop
it stopped to thee in mind
Rigid clouds and mist so high
Where i will see the lullaby
Freed mind, freed thee day
Where i wont be in rain

Published by David Ivancik

Contact: davidivancik@icloud.com

ISBN 979-8-8781-1782-1

Design and composition by David Ivancik

For permission requests, write to the publisher, addressed at davidivancik@icloud.com

First Edition: January 2024